How To Manage Your Money

Key Guidelines For Successful Money Management And Life - How To Develop A Money Mindset And Discipline For Financial Independence

(A Comprehensive Manual On Efficient Time Management And Strategies For Saving Money And Accumulating Wealth)

LadislausKogler

TABLE OF CONTENT

A Chance Walk Along Wall Street.................................... 1

The Study of Spending Psychology 10

Welcome to the Food Truck Universe: 29

Building Self-Respect and Self-Esteem 43

Introduction 66

RESTRICTIONS OF THE 9–5 JOBA 79

Safeguarding Your Money 102

The Benefits of Monitoring Your Spending 127

A Chance WalkAlong Wall Street

The book questions the conventional wisdom on investing and makes the case that the best way to attain long-term financial success is through an index-based, passive investment strategy.

Malkiel starts by saying that it is futile to beat the stock market by active trading or stock selection because it is fundamentally unpredictable. He supports this claim by providing many statistics and anecdotes, demonstrating how even fund managers and expert investors frequently underperform in the market.

Malkiel next presents the idea of a random walk, which denotes that short-term price changes are impossible to forecast accurately and that stock values move randomly in reaction to fresh information. He contends that because of this unpredictability, it is hard, if not impossible, to regularly beat the market through stock selection or active trading.

Malkiel advocates a passive, index-based investing approach, where investors just purchase and keep a diversified portfolio of market-tracking equities or mutual funds. He makes the case that this strategy is less costly, less dangerous, and more successful than stock picking or active trading.

Malkiel offers helpful guidance for putting into practice a passive investment plan throughout the book. He talks about the advantages of tax-efficient investing, the significance of maintaining low expenses, and the benefits of diversity.

Bonds, real estate, and commodities are among the other investing subjects Malkiel covers in several of his chapters. He contends that while these asset classes can be beneficial complements to a well-diversified portfolio, investors should exercise caution when pursuing returns in a single sector.

A fundamental takeaway from the book is how crucial it is to keep a long-term outlook. Malkiel contends that long-term investors should not be concerned with short-term market changes and that attempting to time the market or follow fads is a surefire way to lose money. Rather, he stresses the significance of persevering and upholding a systematic investment approach, especially in market turbulence or unpredictability.

It is an interesting and educational book that questions the conventional wisdom surrounding investment. The book makes the case that the best way to attain long-term financial success is through a passive, index-based investment strategy and offers helpful tips and implementation tactics. Anyone who wants to take charge of their financial future and succeed in long-term investing should read this book.

Top Five Takeaways from the Book Burton Malkiel posits that passive investing is a successful technique because it is grounded in efficient market theory. The book's top five lessons are as follows:

1. The inefficiency of active management: According to Malkiel, active management is a losing tactic used by investors who aim to beat the market by selecting certain stocks or timing the market. He provides data indicating that high fees and transaction costs cause active managers to perform worse than passive index funds over the long run.

2. The significance of diversity: Malkiel highlights the significance of diversification in a portfolio to lower risk. He contends that to have a diversified portfolio, investors need to own a wide. Malkiel suggests low-cost index

fund investing as another way to obtain diversification at a low cost.

3. The fallacy of market timing: Malkiel contends that trying to time the market or forecast when to purchase and sell stocks is pointless. He provides data indicating that investors who attempt to time the market usually underperform it in the long run and that market timing is nearly impossible.

4. The value of comprehending market cycles: Malkiel stresses the significance of comprehending market cycles, which include bull and bear markets, and how they may impact the success of investments. To attain long-term success, he contends that investors should be ready for market downturns and be willing to hang onto their investments through market cycles.

5. The importance of long-term investing: According to Malkiel, the secret to investing success is having a long-term plan. He

advises investing in inexpensive index funds and holding them over time to get market returns. Malkiel urges investors to refrain from acting rashly in response to transient market fluctuations and stresses the value of patience and self-control in investing.

All things considered, "A Random Walk Down Wall Street" provides insightful information about the fundamentals of efficient market theory and the advantages of a passive investing approach. Malkiel's ideas strongly emphasize the ineffectiveness of active management, the benefit of long-term investing, the fallacy of market timing, the significance of diversification, and the relevance of understanding market cycles. Investors who heed Malkiel's counsel can cultivate a patient, disciplined approach to investing that emphasizes long-term success via a diversified, low-cost, and passive investment strategy.

Is debt a good or bad thing?

By taking on some debt, you can attain your goals and accumulate assets for the future.

People often argue that using debt is appropriate when it's used to pay for a home purchase, a start-up business, a reliable car, or education.

However, things aren't always simple. For example, obtaining a certification or degree could result in a higher-paying job with more job security. So, taking out a loan to further your education could be a prudent use of debt.

However, taking on student debt and not finishing the certificate or degree will hinder you rather than help you achieve your goals.

You may keep moving forward and accomplish your goals by taking out a loan for a dependable car to drive you to and from work.

If you borrow all of the value of your cars, then the risk of having multiple cars is worthwhile.

Additionally, if you buy an expensive car, you won't have as much money for other things. It might encourage you to report for duty but also keep you from reaching your financial goals. You and others could make money with a loan to start a business. However, if the business fails, you can find yourself in a situation where you have debt and no way to repay it.

Taking out a loan to buy your house could be a way to accomplish your goals.

However, that debt might put you behind on your payments for a very long period if you cannot make them on time or if you end up owing more than the value of your home.

We are not attempting to scare you with this knowledge. Debt that many people consider to be "positive" needs to be handled carefully.

Some people view credit card debt, payday loans, and pawn loans as "bad" debt since they have fees and interest attached to them, making them unfavourable for consumption purposes like eating out, purchasing presents, or vacationing.

However, you can discover a way to reimburse them for the loan to help you close a cash flow shortfall.

No debt category is, therefore, "good" or "bad." Being aware of your goal or desire for this reason. You can shop for the credit you need before making a final purchase, particularly for larger items like a home or automobile.

You can list all your bills and classify them as secured or unsecured on a debt management worksheet if you default on your loan.

A technique for evaluating more accurate debt is

By examining the resulting percentage, you can ascertain the amount of your income allocated towards debt. A percentage suggests that if you have less money for other things, you might not be as secure financially as you would be.

All other references are to your non-debt needs, desires, and obligations.

Avoiding Debt Pitfalls

If you are taking out a loan to pay for an immediate need, you must avoid going into debt. People in a debt trap often take out additional loans to pay off the debts on their previous loans.

It's a trap because many find it difficult to escape the cycle of taking out loans, piling up debt, and paying them back while still having money left over for necessities like groceries, housing, and transportation.

The Study of Spending Psychology

It dawns on you that not every penny you earn should be spent. You know that you should put something away for a rainy day. However, as the months pass, you discover you cannot maintain your target of investment funds. What's taking place?

It's possible that the brain science of saving money is to blame.

Many different factors are always tugging and prodding at the surface of your consciousness. They might keep you from saving money, even if that's what you want to do.

You have the option to go differently, though. Prepare yourself for what's to come by adhering to a few simple breakthroughs in brain science.

Five Motives It's Difficult to Save Cash

Even though you know it's the proper thing to do, why can't you save money? To address this question, scientists conducted internal and external analyses, and the results they produced may significantly influence how you view your ledger.

For these five main reasons, most people cannot save money.

1. There Is Not Enough of Us

Saving money is difficult when one's income is low. Save enough money for the future, let alone make ends meet.

2. Expenditure Forms Habits

You don't think twice when you see something you need, even though this seems like a sensible decision; when you make the transaction, the pleasure centre of your brain becomes active.

Furthermore, when we come into contact with things like:

Alcohol and Cocaine

Heroin

Our synapses eventually want movement and the hit of synthetics. The necessity can keep us in the purchasing mindset even when our purchases don't save as much as we would have liked.

3. Savings don't pay off right away, but spending money will provide you a boost of joy and a personal item. It can seem like you never get anything when you save money.

If you put money aside in a crisis account, for example, it might help you pay for an unexpected medical bill or a flat tire. You're content to have your investing funds when you need them.

However, if you don't have an urgent need, saving money can make you feel like you're missing out on something you could have right now.

4. It's simple to fall into the trap of believing that only those with money are frugal. Studies suggest that's not always the case, though. For example, the researchers split the subjects into three groups: those who had

money but knew it, those who didn't have money but knew it, and those who didn't have money but knew it. Money was saved by Group 1, which seems to be clear. But group 2 also made financial savings.

Savings are the first step when faced with difficult financial decisions when cuts seem necessary. Still, some save even when their friends do not make that decision. This research indicates that savings practices are more closely related to confidence than money.

5. Like Our Parents, We Save (or Don't Save): According to experts, the "money scripts" we carry around are influenced by our upbringing and the societies in which we reside. Those memories and behavioural patterns influence our decisions when faced with financial decisions, and they do so in a split second.

For example, you may have grown up in a home where:

The savings were uncommon. Most of your family—parents, grandparents, aunts, and uncles—lived paycheck to paycheck.

Spending it was easy. The corner market was open late, and you learned how to shop online before you could read.

Using up all the money was a reward. When your team won a game or received good marks, you achieved your desired outcome.

All those routines and memories influence your decisions when you have to follow a monthly budget. You can decide to spend more money than you save and reduce your savings.

Five Ways to Become an Expert in the Psychology of Financial Savings

Our behaviour is based on the psychology of how we act and respond in various circumstances. Our drives are preprogrammed and quick. But with some self-control and practice, you can change the course and make new decisions.

Take a look at these five great steps.

1. Consistently spend less than you earn

To put it another way, live within your means. Every financial expert will tell you that reducing expenditure is the first step toward saving. If every penny you spend goes toward goods, you won't have any money left for savings. Despite their advice, experts admit it is challenging to take this step.

A budget can be useful. Note down your:

Income. Keep an eye on the amount transferred from your withheld taxes into your account.

Recurring expenses. Remember to pay your rent, utilities, car, and other monthly expenses on time.

Reserved, but not rehashed, expenses. Your budget should also include prepayments for charges, upcoming birthday gifts, event fees, and other similar costs.

Make sure you never owe more than you make by tracking how much you have to spend each month.

2. Encourage Firm Designs for What is about to happen

According to financial experts, anticipating future developments has a greater impact than merely learning about financial concepts. Knowing what you are saving for will help you stay motivated to stick to your resolutions.

Think about your ideal situation in two, five, or ten years. Think about:

Living arrangements. Which would you prefer—having the freedom to rent or buy a home?

Harmony between work and life. Could you work forty hours a week? Conversely, will you cut back on hours or step down?

Familial relationships. Will your parents or kids need your financial assistance?

Treasured possessions. Will you want to buy a new car? New gear for your favourite pastime If you break down these goals into smaller, more achievable tasks, you'll be well on your way to creating a savings habit. If you want a new car in five years, for example, figure out how much you would need to save each month to be able to purchase it without credit.

3. Take Note of Your Small Triumphs

You will begin to meet basic goals once you have solid plans for reserve finances. Tracking and sharing your progress will make you more inclined to follow through on your goal.

Demonstrating progress toward a realistic goal can help you stay motivated and grounded when facing a financial challenge or setback.

Suppose your ambitions will take years to complete. If your goal is to retire by the age of 65, find out how much you would need to save annually by the date of your birthday. When it does, enjoy a little treat—that forbidden bowl of frozen yoghurt—when it appears.

Our Savings Pods will also inspire you. We'll let you know how close you are to reaching the financial goal you've set for your loved ones each time you add cash to your unit. When you log into the application, you can view the fruits of your labour.

4. Automatically Save: Get out of a slump in willpower by automating tasks. You won't be asked to decide whether to put money aside. Rather, you just put the money into savings without a second thought. Saving money automatically is among the greatest and simplest methods to overcome a mental hurdle and move toward a healthier future. You can

meet with you to find out what alternatives are available to you in your area.

Chapter 7: Completing the Picture

The subject of personal finance is intricate. In this chapter, we'll discuss how to combine everything to make a thorough personal finance plan.

Evaluating Your Present Financial Condition

Evaluating your financial status is the first step in creating a personal finance plan. This entails knowing your earnings, outlays, obligations, and possessions. To obtain a clear picture of your financial health, make a net worth statement by taking stock of all your financial accounts.

Establishing Budgetary Objectives

Setting precise financial goals is the next stage after you have a comprehensive picture of your financial status. Your objectives must be attainable, quantifiable, and consistent with your priorities and values. Consider achieving short- and long-term objectives, such as debt repayment, retirement savings, or house ownership.

Making a Spending Plan

One essential tool for reaching your financial objectives is a budget. Make a monthly budget that accounts for your income and outlay, then set aside money for your financial objectives. To stay on track, keep a close eye on your spending and make any necessary adjustments to your budget.

Handling Debt Another crucial component of personal finance is handling Debt. Make a plan to pay off your debts, focusing first on those with high-interest rates. Consider debt consolidation or balance transfers if you want to lower your interest rates.

Investing and Saving

Investing and saving are crucial for creating long-term prosperity. Don't forget to make consistent contributions to your retirement accounts, like an IRA or 401(k). To diversify your investments and increase your profits, consider opening a second investing account.

Safeguarding Your Money

Maintaining your financial stability is essential to achieving your financial objectives. Create an emergency fund, get the right insurance, and take precautions against fraud and identity theft.

Rethinking Your Strategy

Your personal finance plan should be an evolving document that is reviewed frequently and modified as necessary. Plan and make necessary adjustments when your goals are met or your financial condition shifts. Keep up with changes to investment opportunities, tax rules, and other financial aspects that could affect your plan.

How to Quickly Save Money

If you need to start increasing your income quickly, you can perform the following two actions:

Spend less on groceries. One way to boost your income quickly is to cut your shopping expenses, which may be easier than you think. Purchasing fresh produce and other components rather than premade meals may save money. In addition, most grocery stores provide free loyalty programs or rewards cards that get you access to deals and discounts.

Get rid of any unused subscriptions. It is all too easy; you end up with more monthly subscriptions than you use. Even though it can appear, examine your subscriptions with candour. Get rid of any you haven't used in a month or longer! That means you can save more money every month. When the next season of your preferred show airs, you can always reactivate, and if you've finished bingeing, you can always deactivate again. See how your Capital One companion, Eno, can assist you if you require support managing recurring purchases and complimentary samples.

The 30-Day Rule: What Is It?

Struggling to cut back on your indulgences? Think about following the 30-day rule. Give everything you find appealing a month or two before buying it. Then, maybe it's time to buy it if you still want it and it fits your budget. However, you've saved money if you change your mind.

The Final Word

Are you prepared to reduce your Debt and boost your income simultaneously?

Let's start by reviewing your goals. Having a clear financial goal will make creating a plan that gets you there easier.

From there, consider what you spend each month, create a budget, and review your progress often. You may stay focused and upbeat by watching your income grow quickly.

Do you need additional help with your financial journey? Think about making an appointment with a mentor for money and life. You may be able to align your money habits with your lifestyle goals with the assistance of mentors.

8. Database management

Databases can record and assess financial data, provide summaries, identify patterns or trends, and manage a budget. Having database administration expertise allows you to efficiently send account records or charts to administrators, employees, and stakeholders while monitoring expenses. They let you save big data sets, make long-term forecasts and estimates, better manage budgets, and produce visual aids like charts and diagrams to visually represent your data.

9. Making decisions

Managing your budget involves deciding what to prioritize with your earnings and how much to spend. During a project, you can utilize your decision-making abilities to set financial guidelines, such as how much money to give a department and how it will use those funds. A corporation may also benefit from the assistance of budget managers in deciding how to raise capital, make budget reductions, and establish realistic financial goals.

10. Getting Ready

Financial administrators must possess a high degree of readiness. Creating a budget involves identifying the costs of maintaining the firm and defining its goals. A budget manager can use these abilities to assess whether a company has the funds to invest in various operational areas. Accurate financial forecasting and budgeting are encouraged, and budget management processes can be enhanced by excellent budget preparation.

11. A focus on accuracy

While gathering and recording financial data, budget managers pay close attention to every little detail. They precisely record the data to establish financial strategies, make estimates, and manage expenses. To ensure that the budget and journal data accurately represent the funds available in business accounts, meticulous attention is essential when documenting all expenses. Budget managers also use this skill when analyzing financial information and creating reports.

12. Computer proficiency

Administrators of budgets frequently possess excellent technical knowledge and abilities. They could use spreadsheets created by computers to keep track of expenses and assess financial documents. Additionally, they employ specific budgeting software to optimize workflows, like data analysis for precise results applied to budget plans.

Welcome to the Food Truck Universe:

A Delightful Journey Commences

Imagine the enticing attraction of diverse flavours dancing on your taste sensations, the aroma of sizzling bacon wafting through the air, and the lively banter of customers mingling around a colourful truck. This is the magical world of food trucks, my friend. It's a place where your love of food can become a tangible, delectable reality, culinary fantasies come true on wheels, and creativity and innovation are honoured.

I still recall my initial discovery of a food truck event. It was similar to discovering a secret cache of international cuisines. The variety of options, which included handmade ice cream and gourmet sliders, was incredible. The contagious excitement that food trucks brought to the atmosphere got my attention. In the centre of their city, people indulged in an experience, a voyage of tastes, rather than just a meal.

Why Launch a Food Truck Company? A Tasty Route into Entrepreneurship

Let's conclude: Why should you consider launching a food truck company? Well, my buddy, there's a world of possibility waiting for you beyond the mouthwatering food and lively atmosphere. Above all, it's an opportunity to transform your love of cooking into a successful business. Do you recall the recipes you've mastered over time? The ones that give your family and friends the creeps? Imagine serving those to an ever-increasing group, witnessing the joy on people's faces, and knowing that you are the source of those moments of absolute gastronomic ecstasy.

Moreover, launching a food truck company is a path to independence. Bid farewell to the routine of working from 9 to 5, and welcome to a schedule that you can customise. You're more than simply a cook—you're an innovator in your field of cooking and a creative and business owner. Not to mention the money opportunity. Turning your passion into a profitable business is possible with a well-run food truck, as they have lower overhead costs than regular eateries.

Are You a Good Fit for a Food Truck? The Phase of Soul-Searching

Let's have an open discussion before you start designing your food truck and honing your unique dish. Is a food truck the best career choice for you? It's not only about preparing a feast and waiting for the crowds to form. It involves a lot of effort, long hours, and multitasking as a chef, marketer, and strategist, among other things. But every struggle has its own set of benefits, I assure you.

Consider what motivates you to launch a food truck. What excites you more: cooking for others, starting your own business, or having the flexibility to pursue what you love? Can you manage the day-to-day operations, legal requirements, and the odd snag of running a business? You're headed in the correct direction if your passion outshines your doubts and anxieties.

Main Advantages and Difficulties: Food Truck Life's Positive and Negative Aspects

Like any great culinary creation, the food truck industry has its unique flavour combination, including sweet and spicy elements. Let's start by discussing the advantages. Flexibility is key; you choose where to open your store—from busy street corners to outdoor music festivals. The tight-knit food truck community is quite helpful, offering advice and companionship. Additionally, compared to traditional restaurants, the overhead costs are far lower, providing greater financial flexibility.

Still, there are obstacles in the way. You're servicing clients rain or shine, but the weather may be unpredictable. Furthermore, although rivalry can inspire innovation, it can also result in people vying for attention in a crowded area. But remember that these difficulties are merely a part of the journey that adds to the satisfaction of success.

Thus, when you set out on this gastronomic journey, remember to keep your aspirations low and your resolve high. Launching a food truck company is similar to making a sophisticated dish: it calls for the correct components, cautious preparation, and a dash of magic. But have no fear—this guide will walk you through every stage, providing advice, pointers, and a dash of inspiration from people who have been there and done that. Prepare to enjoy the trip ahead; it will be delicious.

. Recognise your influence

We are forced to take charge of our lives when we know what we want. We no longer dwell on the unpleasant aspects of the world and the reasons behind our inability to achieve our desired goals. Rather, we are admitting that we have powerful control over our destiny. Utilising our strengths, we must discover and embody who we are.

According to Dr. Firestone, people's power is based on the strength, skill, and confidence they progressively acquire. Finding love, fulfilment, and purpose in interpersonal connections is a healthy, natural need. Realising our enormous influence on our lives is a necessary step towards grasping our power. We are the creators of the environment in which we live. To improve the world, one must reject the victim mentality, embrace empowerment, and adopt a new outlook.

Dr. Robert Firestone has expanded his list of the "6 Aspects of Being an Adult" with more instances.

1. Allow your emotions to guide you, but use logic to guide your decisions.

2. Establish goals and take the required actions to reach them.

3. Take charge and try to stand up for yourself rather than being dependent and submissive.

4. Make an effort to interact equally with others.

5. Show an open mind to new ideas and welcome constructive criticism.

6. Acquire total command over all facets of your conscious life.

5. Calm Down Your Inner Judge

As adults, we must give up using self-soothing or self-punishing as a self-parenting strategy. To put it in Dr., A judgmental mindset that tells us we aren't worthy of what we want or aren't good enough to attain it, or a soothing mindset that suggests we don't need to try or that we just need to be taken care of, could be the components of this harmful thought process. By identifying and vanquishing this inner enemy, we learn to become stronger and more capable of realising our genuine selves rather than being overbearing or immature. According to mindfulness specialist Dr. Donna Rockwell, the goal is to subdue the doubting mind by disarming negative thoughts to reach the "state of upliftedness that makes everything else possible—that provides the "go for it!" energy we crave."

6. Exhibit charity and goodwill

Mahatma Gandhi once said that losing oneself in the service of others is the best way to find yourself.

Generosity not only prolongs life and improves physical and mental health, but it also helps boost one's feeling of purpose and gives lives greater significance and meaning. According to studies, giving makes individuals happier than receiving. To find our way in life, it is helpful to embrace a compassionate mindset towards ourselves and others and to practise generosity as a mental health philosophy. People are often content when they have altruistic goals. These folks are kind and considerate towards others. You go about your day as usual, trying to maintain a COAL attitude—which Dr. Daniel Siegel defines as being inquisitive, receptive, accepting, and loving of who you are and your unique journey—as you do so.

7. Appreciate the value of friendship

Although we often think that our family defines who we are, our families are not something we choose. Even if we don't always get to choose how we spend our childhood, as adults, we can choose who and what we want to be when we grow up and create the family we desire. We may seek out those who make us happy, support the things that make us feel good about ourselves, and renew our enthusiasm for life. Of course, this family may consist of our relatives, but its main members are the people we consider to be devoted friends and allies. Building this family is necessary to discover oneself because our interactions with others are greatly influenced by the people we choose to surround ourselves with. Having a network of people who believe in us promotes personal development and helps us reach our objectives.

Overview

The process of effectively planning, arranging, and regulating your free time to increase output, accomplish objectives, and lessen stress is known as time management. It is a necessary skill for people and organisations who wish to maximise their time and complete their duties. The following are some methods for efficient time management:

First, make sure well-defined objectives guide your everyday actions. Keeping your attention on the important things. Second, assign tasks a priority. Determine which activities are most crucial and urgent, then prioritise them. To ascertain the order of importance, apply strategies such as the Eisenhower Matrix.

Make a schedule and set aside time to organise your daily, weekly, or monthly tasks. Make a realistic schedule, assign tasks, and make a to-do list. By doing this, you'll be able to maintain organisation and stop wasting time on unimportant chores.

Get rid of distractions, determine which ones impact your productivity most, and take action to reduce them. When required, find a quiet place free from interruptions, turn off your phone's needless notifications, and restrict how much time you spend on social media during work.

If at all feasible, assign work that others can complete. This enables you to concentrate your time and efforts on tasks that need your attention.

Instead of attempting to multitask, practice time blocking by organising related tasks into blocks of time. Set aside time, for instance, to respond to emails, schedule meetings, etc. This boosts productivity and lessens distractions.

Employ productivity strategies. The Pomodoro Technique is one strategy that has you working for predetermined amounts of time—typically 25 minutes—and then pausing for a brief respite. You can become more efficient and maintain attention by using these strategies.

Regularly review your time management practices and make any necessary improvements. Determine time-wasting habits or places for improvement, then adjust your daily schedule and preparation accordingly.

Recall that effective time management is a skill that needs discipline and repetition. You can become more proficient at efficiently managing your time and increasing your output with practice.

Online platforms and the gig economy: There are many ways to make money with your time, thanks to the growth of these two industries. You can provide services on a flexible basis, such as driving, housework, freelance work, or specialised expertise, through platforms like TaskRabbit, Upwork, Fiverr, and Uber. These platforms allow you to leverage your skills and time to make money.

Recall that discovering alternatives for earning money in your free time necessitates assessing your abilities, passions, and market niche. It's critical to determine whether there is a market for your services, establish competitive pricing, and always look for methods to improve your value proposition and skill set. To optimise your earning potential and preserve a positive work-life balance, time management and sensible prioritisation are also essential.

Building Self-Respect and Self-Esteem

Self-esteem is "belief and trust in your worth and ability."

Let's examine each definitional word in turn:

Belief: The feeling of having faith and assurance in your skills. Being aware of your worth and significance.

Ability: The mental or physical capacity required to carry out a task.

Not just one good quality, but all of these characteristics and attitudes are necessary for having self-esteem. Ideally, you would possess these qualities to truly feel good about yourself.

Why High School Students Need to Feel Good About Themselves

If you have a strong feeling of self-worth and self-confidence in your talents, you will fully enjoy your time as a high school student. Your total well-being will be greatly impacted by your capacity to bring all the many aspects of your life together into an "ease" condition where you feel content and self-assured in all you can do.

You'll feel empowered to take on new tasks and grow individually to become your best self after you are free of crushing self-doubts.

What precisely is a lack of self-worth?

Self-worth isn't

❖ Having conceit in your abilities.

❖ Putting others around you down to make yourself feel better.

❖ Owning a large amount of wealth and belongings

Being arrogant and indifferent.

❖ Exhibiting a pompous demeanour.

❖ Feeling proud

The True Significance of Self-Respect

1. Being sincere

Imagine not feeling obligated to behave in a particular way. It is not expected of you to fit in or win people over. Since everyone can see the real, you imagine not having to put on a show, doubt who you are, or mistrust other people.

It must feel amazing and liberating. A person with a strong sense of self-worth is confident in who they are and understands that they don't have to alter to fit in.

They don't give societal conventions or standards much thought because they are content with who they are. Please be advised that this does not mean they are breaking social norms.

2. being aware of your objectives and self.

Finding your true passion and purpose in life is possible with confidence. It is beneficial for long-term planning. You can improve your social relationships and academic performance if you are confident in your abilities.

If you like, you might also focus your life on a particular interest or passion.

3. Decision-Making Clarity

Strong self-worth and self-esteem make a person adept at choosing and following through on decisions. They trust the judgment they make. They know their requirements and objectives and can plan for the future.

4. Keeping an optimistic mindset

It will be easier for you to understand others if you know yourself and your perspective on the world. It also implies that you can acknowledge the limitations of yourself and others.

Excess self-blame is unnecessary because you are willing to accept that you are not always correct and that other people can make mistakes.

5. Recognizing Your Value.

Acknowledging your worth as a high school student is essential to accepting oneself as a valuable member of society. It implies you won't settle for anything less than what you deserve.

You won't value yourself if you've spent your entire life believing you're a failure or, worse, hearing it from others. You are worthy of a happy life.

If you believe that, you'll come to believe that you are undeserving of love, happiness, and other things, and you'll withdraw into a bubble of poor self-esteem and value.

6. Proficiency in Efficient Communication.

When asked about their ideas, most high school pupils with strong self-esteem can respond intelligently and explain. They can communicate their underlying values and the reasoning for their convictions because they consistently act according to who they truly are.

They are free to convey who and what they are since they are not trying to be someone they are not, and they are not obliged to respond or offer explanations.

7. possessing a success-driven worldview.

People with a strong sense of value and self-worth are highly motivated to achieve in everything they undertake. It's the understanding that if you know who you are, you'll also know your advantages and disadvantages. It's not hubris.

8. the capacity to establish wholesome relationships.

Building and maintaining healthy connections is simpler if you're not putting an undue burden on yourself by trying to be someone you're not, personally and professionally.

Being true to oneself is all that matters. Knowing, loving, and understanding oneself can help you connect with others deeper—even though this may seem apparent.

Being genuine in interpersonal interactions fosters trust, which is a more crucial component than maintaining an act since healthy relationships are based on reciprocal trust.

9. being prepared and eager to help.

Have you ever observed that those with a strong sense of value and self-worth frequently volunteer to assist others first?

These are typically volunteers, committee members, and others who are prepared to make sacrifices for the good of others. These people wish to share their happiness because they are content with their lives.

10. Accepting novel challenges

You are more likely to take on new tasks if you have faith in your skills, beliefs, and self since you won't be held back by the debilitating "fear of failure" feeling.

Rather, you will realize that the only way to determine whether you are very good at something is to try it out. If you're average at something, it won't be viewed as a failure; rather, it will be recognized as a lesson gained.

Section 1

Recognizing your spending patterns

What spending patterns do you have?

The patterns in how you spend your money are known as your spending habits. Many factors, including your income, lifestyle, values, and financial objectives, might impact them.

Typical expenditure patterns include the following:

● Impulsive spending: Consistently spending money without giving it much thought on items you don't need or want.

Spending money to deal with stress, grief, or other emotions is known as emotional spending.

● Spending under peer pressure: Investing cash to stay up with friends or coworkers.

● Spending money on activities you do without giving it much thought, like getting coffee every morning, is habitual spending.

How do you keep tabs on your expenses?

Towards comprehending your spending patterns. This entails recording every purchase you make, regardless of size. Numerous methods exist for keeping tabs on your expenditures, including:

● Using a budgeting app: You may track your expenditure with a variety of budgeting apps that are accessible. Usually, these apps let you link credit cards and bank accounts so you can view all of your transactions in one location.

● Maintaining a spending notebook: You can maintain a spending journal to track your expenditures by hand. Record all your financial transactions, including the date, amount, and purchase category.

● Spreadsheet tracking: Spreadsheets can also be used to keep tabs on your expenditures. If you want to have more control over how your money is allocated, this is a fantastic alternative.

Which are the various spending categories?

You can recognize your many spending categories once you have recorded your expenditures. Typical expenditure categories consist of:

● Housing: Property taxes, utilities, and rent or a mortgage.

● Food and dining covers supermarkets, eateries, and delivery services.

● transit: This covers the cost of petrol, auto insurance, and public transit.

● Insurance: This includes homes, vehicles, and health insurance.

● Debt payments: These comprise payments for credit cards, auto loans, and education loans.

● Entertainment: This covers motion pictures, live performances, and athletic events.

● Personal care: This encompasses clothing, toiletries, and haircuts.

● Investments and savings refer to the cash you set aside for retirement or other financial objectives.

Here are some more pointers to help you begin investing:

● Get knowledgeable. Better decisions will genuinely be what you wish to make the more you are comfortable contributing. Numerous publications, websites, and courses are available to demonstrate your contribution.

● Start small. You don't need much money to start managing your finances. Financial planning can be started with any amount, even as little as ~$50 a month.

● Make consistent investments. After a while, the best method to cultivate your abundance is to make continuous contributions. This means spending a small amount of money regularly, perhaps once a month or yearly, for efficient financial planning.

● Spread out your holdings. Avoid keeping all of your resources in one location. Distribute your money over various projects and resource categories to reduce your risk.

- Regularly adjust your portfolio. It addresses your difficulties as your financial situation changes.

Over time, investing can be a terrific way to increase your money, but you should always be aware that risk is involved. Educate yourself on investing and select investments based on your investment objectives and risk tolerance.

Chapter 5: The Conventional Approach to Retirement

An unidentified source stated (McGough, 2023). This should provoke thinking in all of us, especially the younger generation. Bosses typically anticipate when you plan to retire, but you can surprise them earlier. In the past few decades, almost everyone retired via traditional methods. This chapter will provide you with all the required knowledge to comprehend this method and learn how to modify it for your early retirement plan. We'll also talk about inflation and how it affects your retirement.

Growing Prices: The Quiet Tax

Looking back five years, consider what you could have purchased with a $10 bill. Ask yourself, "Can I still buy the same item for $10 or less?" in the present. The item in question has likely become more expensive, meaning the $10 has lost its value. How come this would be the case? The reason for this is the idea of inflation, which approximates the significance.

The effect of inflation on your money will be better understood by looking at the example below. Let's say you have $10 saved up to buy milk. Milk will cost $1.25 a litre if you buy it now, translating to eight litres. Buying enough milk to make 32 cups of coffee excites you. But when you try to make the same purchase a year later, the price per litre has unfortunately increased to $1.50. You can now only buy six litres of milk with your $10 instead of eight. The production expense and the demand for milk increased the price per litre.

A few months into the Russia-Ukraine conflict in 2022, you might have noticed something similar to this inflationary effect when you stopped at a petrol station to fill up your car. It's critical to comprehend how inflation impacts your retirement funds and assets. You'll see that a price increase is not the same as inflation. While price increases can happen over short or lengthy periods, inflation is the general increase in prices of goods and services over extended periods. Inflation also considers price fluctuations for bulk purchases of goods and services, such as fuel, groceries, and electricity. Inflation may happen even if the prices of some of these goods and services rise and those of others fall.

Price adjustments are brought about by variations in the cost of production or the demand for products and services. The creation of money is one of the main causes of inflation in the contemporary era.

In the past, any printed money had to be backed by an equivalent physical item, such as silver or gold, stored in a vault. This isn't the case with the careless way money is printed these days. Since then, the government has been able to issue money whenever it pleases. A nation's currency weakens due to an increase in the amount of money in its financial system because of this increased currency supply. This indicates that inflation is rising, and today's money is worth less than it was a few years ago.

Methods for Computing Inflation

by most nations, including Spain, the United States, and other European nations, to calculate inflation. This index is typically computed over a minimum of a year, although month-to-month comparisons are possible. The computation seeks to depict changes in the cost of products and services for most of the nation's citizens.

The important thing to understand is that the CPI is an average and does not represent your inflation. Because of this, there's a good chance that your inflation is greater than normal. For instance, the average CPI in the United States from 1960 to 2022 was 3.8% annually; nevertheless, yours may be as high as 5% or even 10% (WorldData.info, n.d.). Your lifestyle and the kinds of things you often buy will determine how much inflation you experience. It is worthwhile to determine your own CPI in light of the actual items and services you use. Monthly pricing data required to generate the Consumer Pricing Index (CPI) can be found at the National Statistics Institute in Spain.

Before gathering pricing information:

List the products and services you frequently buy.

For easier organizing and computations, compile this data into a spreadsheet.

After obtaining this data, gather pricing information for the month and the equivalent months twelve months prior.

For instance, you would gather data from July of this year and July of last year if your most recent CPI data pertains to July.

Once you've gathered all the required information, compute each item's inflation over the preceding 12 months using the CPI formula below:

CPI = ((Y − X)/X) x 100 is the inflation rate, where Y is the item's current price, and X is its price from a year ago.

It should be noted that base figures, which are relative prices of goods and services compared to the price given at a value of 100 in a chosen year, might be used in place of actual prices for goods and services.

Let me demonstrate how to determine the CPI for meat in the United States between June 2022 and June 2023. The base price of meats was 316.110 in June 2022 and 315.561 in June 2023.

CPI = -0.549/316.110 x 100 = -0.2% ((315.561 - 316.110)/316.110) x 100

For every other item, perform the same computation once again. Once done, find your weighted average inflation over the interest period by averaging your commodities and services. Here's an example of how to figure out how much each item contributes to your average inflation:

Let's say that your entire expenses for a certain July month come to $2,000. For a $20 bottle of milk, you want to determine how much inflation contributed to your average personal inflation. Your average personal inflation will be 0.05% (5% x $20/$2,000 = 0.05%) if you spend $20 on milk. To find your average personal inflation, follow the same procedure for expenses and sum the outcomes.

Because the things you buy might not be the same as those included in your country's inflation computation, your inflation will differ from the average inflation in your country.

Regarding inflation, there is only one conclusion: Your investment returns are diminished by the silent tax. Soon, you can monitor how inflation has affected your assets. First, according to WorldData.info (n.d.-a), this is the historical inflation for Spain and the United States from 2013 to 2022.

U.S. Spain

2022 8.00% 8.4%

2021 3.1% 4.7%

2020 1.2% - 0.03%

2019: 1.8% 0.7%

2018: 2.4%; 1.68 percent

2.1% 1.96% in 2017

1.3% - 0.2% in 2016

2015: 0.1% to 0.5%

2014: 1.6% - 0.2%

2013: 1.5%; 1.4%

Compared to the United States, Spain experienced deflation more frequently throughout the ten years of interest. Inflation affected both countries most of the time.

Calculating investments will show that actual returns decrease and real returns rise when inflation occurs. For example, if an investment yields 9% over a given period and inflation is 2% annually, the actual return is 7% (9% - 7% = 2% yearly). This implies that your investment should yield at least 11% over the same period if you desire a yearly return of 9%. When the effects of taxes are considered, the situation can appear much more dire!

Many people avoid performing the necessary computations because they realize earning investment returns that beat inflation might be more difficult. The problem is that this isn't helpful since their financial circumstances remain the same. They bury their heads in the sand, thinking things will improve financially. It takes guts to face the music of your finances, and I suppose it takes fortitude to face reality.

Numerous investments are available, some of which outperform inflation while others underperform it. After accounting for taxes and inflation, the performance of two US investments is shown in the table below:

Investment return before taxes and inflation Income tax return at 22% Average return after taxes and inflation is 2.4%

1.85% 1.44% -0.96% iShares S&P GSCI Commodity-Indexed Trust (1.44% - 2.4% = -0.96%)

7.5% 5.85% 3.45% Real estate investment trust (REIT)

(The amounts above are hypothetical; they were selected to highlight how taxes and inflation affect your investment returns.)

The above table illustrates how your money loses purchasing power when an investment performs worse than inflation. An improved situation would be if your post-tax returns showed a profit and exceeded inflation. The issue is that you cannot make enough money to retire comfortably and be young.

Introduction

Many newly licensed real estate agents don't make it through their first two years. It might be disastrous to overestimate revenue in addition to underestimating expenses. Others overly rely on antiquated industry cliches in the real estate sector, which has expanded online since the Great Recession.

If you know when to follow the crowd and when to try new strategies, it will be easier for you to launch a prosperous real estate business from the start.

11. As a recently licensed real estate agent, you should invest in yourself by attending seminars and pursuing further education: Online courses in social media marketing, finance, and general business are just a few. You may stay current on the latest real estate trends and join local networking

groups by subscribing to the newsletters of different real estate websites. If you are a member of the National Association of Realtors (NAR), set aside some time to read the studies and publications that the organization publishes.

12. Get ready for open houses: Choose a date for your open house that does not coincide with any holidays, neighbourhood gatherings, or local festivals. Start working with the homeowner to stage their house at least one week beforehand. Give the owner a to-do list so they may assist with any last-minute maintenance, organizing, and cleaning tasks. You might also want to employ a deep cleaner to thoroughly clean the property if you have the time and money to do so.

Arrive early on the open house day, so you have time to explore the area and hunt for strange objects. During this period, you may also put up refreshments, prepare your marketing materials, turn on all the lights, open the blinds and curtains, play some music, and turn on all the lights.

13. Getting involved in your community: Getting involved in your community is a great way to build your network. You should consider volunteering for a nonprofit, joining a civic group, and participating in neighbourhood fundraisers. Helping your community and those in need can help you develop trust with locals, enhance recommendations, and generate leads for your business.

14. Build a rapport with your clients: Successful real estate agents understand how important it is to build trusting bonds with prospective customers. An essential aspect of your work is ensuring the customer feels comfortable, cared for, and understood. Make eye contact, practice active listening, and ask plenty of questions to develop trust with your

clients. Look for methods to assist your clients and express your gratitude to them. Building trusting relationships with your clients can help with cooperation and boost referrals.

15. Using excellent photos: You may sell properties faster and potentially draw in more potential buyers with the help of your house listings and marketing materials. Having a professional photographer take pictures of your listings can help you save time and set them out from other houses for sale. Over time, you may utilize these photos to build an impressive portfolio and improve your marketing collateral, which might lead to more sellers selecting you to represent them in real estate transactions.

To put it simply, real estate is:

Real estate includes any natural or artificial features such as buildings, dwellings, fences, bridges, water, trees, minerals, and any long-term improvements affixed to the ground.

Real estate is one category of real property. On the other hand, personal property includes anything that isn't fixed to the ground permanently, such as vehicles, boats, jewellery, furnishings, and farm equipment.

Although it can be dangerous and challenging, real estate investing can succeed. Property management, joint partnerships, and wholesaling are a few ways real estate investors might profit. It also takes some insight to succeed in this fiercely competitive sector.

While a degree isn't always required to succeed in real estate investing, investors may find general courses and discipline programs some universities offer helpful. Superb real estate investors, whether or not they hold a degree, typically share a few characteristics.

3) Professionally Promotes Your House

The realtor's skills go beyond what is required; they can also sell a client's house.

Home sellers want agents who are good at marketing their properties.

You can rely on your realtor to know how to arrange your house for a professional photo session if you want top-notch marketing materials to highlight your property. That is most convenient for them.

While several local "micro-influencers" will use social media to draw in customers, most will also employ other tried-and-true traditional and digital marketing techniques, such as the Multiple Listing Service (MLS).

When listing agents assist with advertising, their properties can sell 34.7% faster than For Sale By Owner (FSBO) properties.

4) Clear and constant communication

In addition to selling a house fast and for a good price, a competent real estate agent will make the process fun. The most important difference between the two is their ability to communicate effectively.

Maintaining effective communication is one of the hardest things to learn for professionals. Real estate agents are not any different. Home sellers must stay in close contact with their agent throughout the process to ensure they feel comfortable.

As a home seller, you are attempting to balance the craziness of selling a house and your regular life. While the realtor is working to sell your house, you cannot afford to be kept in the dark about what is happening behind the scenes, and you do not have time to handle misunderstandings.

This is the reason it's so important to do pre-interview interviews with your realtors. It's important to learn not only about your realtor's methods for selling your house but also their communication style.

5) Establishes priorities Before Asset Allocation and Risk Tolerance

Evaluation of Risk Tolerance

Evaluate the combined risk tolerance of the two of you. To what extent do you find the idea of swings in investments acceptable? Do you both favour a more cautious strategy with lesser risk or are you both ready to take on more risk to earn larger returns? Determining your asset allocation requires knowing how much risk you can tolerate.

Asset Distribution

The process of allocating your investments among several asset classes, including cash, bonds, and stocks, is known as asset allocation. Reflected in your asset allocation. A well-balanced portfolio can assist you in accomplishing your goals and successfully managing risk.

Spreading Out Your Investments for Diversification

One essential component of wise investing is diversification. It entails distributing your assets over various sectors, markets, and geographical areas. By diversifying, you can increase the stability and resilience of your portfolio by lessening the impact of a single investment's bad performance.

Juggling Benefits and Risk

You and your partner must choose the degree of diversity that best suits your goals and risk tolerance while balancing risk and return. Aiming for long-term growth, your diverse portfolio should be built to withstand market swings.

Investment Accounts and Vehicles

Selecting Investment Funds

Think about the kinds of investment accounts that complement your collaborative investing approach. These could include tax-advantaged accounts such as 401(k)s, individual retirement accounts (IRAs), joint brokerage accounts, or other retirement funds. Selecting accounts that align with your strategy is important because your selection may have tax ramifications.

Contributions and Continual Evaluation

Choose a strategy for consistently adding to your investing portfolio. Long-term growth requires contributions to be made consistently. Plan recurring evaluations as a pair to evaluate the performance of your portfolio, rebalance as necessary, and make modifications in response to shifts in your financial circumstances or objectives.

Establishing a collaborative investment plan is crucial in realizing your financial goals together. It guarantees that your investing philosophies coincide and offers a plan for jointly increasing your money.

Overview

It's not only a notion that you have. You have kindling that has the potential to grow into something enormous and revolutionary. You're getting ready to leap into entrepreneurship, a trip that not everyone is brave enough to do. So, let's start by giving you a round of applause!

Now that you have a brilliant concept, you find yourself at a fork in the road where many difficult choices must be made. Selecting the appropriate business structure is one of the process's most crucial—yet often ignored—steps. This choice serves as your guide, the framework for your company's growth and development. Plotting your business's course, protecting your interests, and outlining your financial plan are just as important as placing your name on a sign.

This book serves as your reliable wilderness guide in this situation. It will guide you through the maze-like maze of corporate structures like a beacon. We'll go beyond the surface, from the independent Sole Proprietors to the cooperative Limited Liability Companies. These structures by the time you flip the last page of chapter one.

However, there is one form that is frequently chosen by new and small enterprises: the S Corporation. And we're going to focus our spotlight there. Together, we'll take a deep dive into the S Corporation's core values, examining its fascinating features and comprehending why it can be the piece that completes your company's puzzle.

We delve even further into the S Corporation in chapter two. Why ought you to give it some thought? What benefits do you see? What is its relative performance to other structures? And the crucial query: does it make sense for your company? Fear not—we'll delve into the details and provide answers to all of these questions.

Are you in favour of forming an S Corporation? The third chapter is your toolkit. It will help you understand the legal jargon, walk you through filling out forms, and navigate the state.

Now that your S Corporation is airborne, you must properly navigate it. Chapter Four enters the picture here. It will guide you through every step of managing your business, including organizing your team, keeping track of finances, adhering to legal requirements, and looking for expansion prospects.

In chapter five, money talks. Here, we'll explain the special tax advantages of an S Corporation, discuss methods to increase your tax deductions, offer helpful advice for managing tax season, and even reveal a few closely held accounting secrets.

We'll also be there when it's time to close your S Corporation. In Chapter Six, you will learn how to dissolve a business, recognize when it's time to hang up your hat as an entrepreneur and understand the tax ramifications. There will never be any darkness for you.

Realm of corporate entities and their interactions. This book is prepared to be your reliable resource for making confident, knowledgeable choices. Let's get our hands dirty, get started, and clear the path for your entrepreneurial success story.

RESTRICTIONS OF THE 9-5 JOBA

As an experienced entrepreneur who has seen success, I can assure you that exchanging time for money is very common. It's a simple deal where you provide your knowledge and experience in return for a fixed monthly salary or an hourly rate. But here's the thing, buddy: there are limitations to this strategy. Most of the time, how much money you can make depends on how many hours you can work. Therefore, it's time to look beyond the clock and consider more creative routes to riches to achieve greater financial freedom!

Let's face it: accumulating riches is not an easy task. It requires patience, hard work, and an openness to trying out novel approaches that fit your circumstances. There isn't a single strategy that works for everyone. Still, one thing is certain: investing in long-term income-generating assets and developing passive income streams are key components of building long-term wealth. You may design a long-term, sustainable wealth-building strategy that isn't constrained by the number of hours in a day by changing your emphasis from only exchanging time for money to developing a portfolio of income-generating assets.

9 to 5 occupations have a lot of downsides, some of which are as follows:

Restricted income potential: How much money you can make when you exchange your time for money is determined by how many hours you can work. This is because time is a limited resource, and the money you can make will always be capped regardless of how many hours you work. Long hours may enable you to make more money soon, but they are not a long-term or scalable answer.

Lack of flexibility: Working a regular 9–5 job means committing to a fixed schedule, making it difficult to take care of personal obligations or pursue other hobbies. Because of the rigidity of a 9–5 job, you might not have the time or energy to pursue hobbies or engage in things you are passionate about after a long day at work.

Lack of job security: The stability that full-time jobs formerly offered has become questionable in today's dynamic economy. Many workers are exposed to the risk of being let go or losing their jobs without warning. People struggling to maintain their living and make ends meet may experience a significant deal of stress and worry as a result. Outsourcing and automation have made even employment that was considered safe and secure vulnerable.

Restricted prospects for advancement: 9–5 occupations might not offer many chances for advancement, which could make workers feel stuck in their careers and unable to realize their full potential. In certain fields, there are few opportunities for job promotion, and you can spend years in one position with no room to grow.

Restricted control over your work: In 9–5 positions, you frequently have little influence over your work or the projects you're given. This might be upsetting because, even though you could have a certain set of skills or be passionate about a subject, your employer might put you on projects that don't fit these descriptions. When you work for someone else, their priorities, expectations, and vision govern your work. You can feel like you're merely going through the motions with little direction or purpose, resulting in a lack of creativity, inspiration, and contentment.

Limited work-life balance: Being on call all the time or working long hours can hurt your personal life and cause stress and burnout.

Reduced autonomy and creativity: Working for someone else may restrict your freedom to be creative or take chances with your work. Being stuck in a job that does not fulfil them or correspond with their personal goals or beliefs is common. People end up with occupations that they don't like or don't provide them with a sense of fulfilment, which causes them to feel frustrated and unsatisfied.

Many people have succeeded in pursuing alternative vocations or entrepreneurial pursuits after bravely quitting their 9-5 jobs. These tales demonstrate that there is room for financial success and personal contentment outside the conventional 9-5 schedule.

But it's crucial to understand that jumping might have dangers and problems. It necessitates being prepared to venture beyond your comfort zone, face uncertainty, and accept the possibility of failing. Establishing a profitable company or choosing an unconventional professional path demands commitment, perseverance, and a readiness to change and grow as you go.

Nevertheless, there can be enormous benefits for those prepared to take risks, including the ability to follow their passions with freedom and autonomy, unrestricted financial growth, and a greater sense of personal fulfilment. Realizing your dreams requires you to be prepared to take calculated risks and do the necessary work.

Numerous accounts abound of people quitting their 9-5 employment to launch their companies and find tremendous success. Here are a handful of instances:

Sara Blakely: Sara Blakely founded Spanx, a women's underwear firm that has become a well-known worldwide brand after quitting her sales career. Blakely is now a billionaire.

Daymond John: Daymond John founded FUBU, a fashion brand that has become a household name after quitting his work as a server. Today, John is a prosperous businessman, financier, and television personality, best known for his work on the popular program Shark Tank.

Oprah Winfrey: After quitting her work as a news anchor, Oprah Winfrey launched The

Oprah Winfrey Show, a talk show that went on to become one of the most popular in television history. These days, Winfrey is a media tycoon, philanthropist, and cultural figure.

Jan Koum: After leaving his position at Yahoo, Jan Koum founded WhatsApp, a messaging service that has become one of the most popular means of communication worldwide. For $19 billion, Koum eventually sold WhatsApp to Facebook.

These tales show how taking risks and pursuing your business may lead to enormous success.

✐ Mentality adjustments for monetary prosperity

An effective strategy for reaching financial success is changing one's perspective. It begins with realizing that our capacity to reach our objectives can greatly impact how we see money and success. You can unintentionally undermine your attempts to attain financial prosperity, for instance, if you think wealth is the domain of the chosen few or the source of all evil. On the other side, you're more likely to take the required actions to attain financial success if you adopt a growth mindset and think that anyone can succeed financially with effort, commitment, and a readiness to learn and adapt. The following significant mental adjustments can assist you in reaching your financial objectives:

From scarcity to abundance: Many individuals approach money with the idea that only so much wealth is available to them. Feelings of worry, competitiveness, and fear may result from this. You can realize that you can generate your riches and that there is an abundance of wealth and opportunities available to you by adopting an abundance mindset.

Individuals with fixed mentality think they are stuck with their skills and abilities and incapable of changing or getting better. Feelings of helplessness and insufficient motivation may result from this. Conversely, a growth mindset acknowledges that practice and dedication may enhance and refine our skills and aptitudes.

From consumer to creator: Many individuals treat money like a consumer, immediately blowing their earnings on items that make them feel good. Changing your perspective to one of a creator can assist you in realizing that you are capable of producing wealth and adding worth rather than merely consuming it.

Transitioning from short-term to long-term thinking: Many people concentrate on short-term gains and instant gratification rather than considering their long-term financial goals. You can see that disciplined saving, investing, and postponing gratification can pay off in the long run by adopting a long-term thinking approach.

From fear to empowerment: Many individuals worry about debt, bills, and financial responsibilities regarding money. You can recognize that you have power over your financial circumstances and that you can take action to make them better by adopting an empowered mentality.

By implementing these mental changes, you may improve your financial success and take a more proactive and optimistic approach to managing your money.

Naturally, it takes time, work, and a willingness to question your financial assumptions and beliefs to establish a proactive and constructive financial attitude. But if you work hard and are persistent, you can start managing your money and building a better, more affluent future for your family and yourself.

TRILOGY

Keeping your body clean is essential to stay healthy and shield yourself from needless infections and illnesses. Although this may sound drastic (and nasty), good cleanliness habits can help avoid conditions like worms, diarrhoea, scabies, lice, and tooth decay.

Maintaining cleanliness is also a social obligation. It makes sense that you wouldn't want someone to smell you before they saw you. You may engage in social interactions with freedom and confidence when you take good care of your physique.

Your body is also undergoing a great deal of change. For instance, numerous hormonal changes occur, which may cause hair growth in previously unnoticed body areas. You might notice a change in the way your body smells. It is indeed manageable with appropriate hygiene.

Maintaining cleanliness fosters discipline. Getting out of bed in the morning, showering, brushing your teeth, taking care of yourself, and so on requires work. You'll reap the benefits of developing a consistent self-care routine for years to come if you start now!

One word for it: changes!

Alright, you've heard about puberty before. Has varying durations and begins at different times. Boys and girls can start between the ages of 10 and 14, whereas girls usually start between ages 8 and 13. Since each of us is different, this is only a general trend.

Here, a lot is happening. And while this is a significant aspect of puberty, it's not physical. Your body will feel and behave differently due to hormonal signals from your brain to your body.

Boys and females go through puberty differently, but similarly. Both experience some changes, such as the emergence of underarm and pubic hair, a shift in body odour, and the dreaded zits. Additionally, certain changes—like ejaculation and menstrual periods—will occur. Boys will note that their voices change and that hair grows on their faces. Girls report larger emotional swings and the enlargement of their breasts.

This is a typical period of life that we must all experience to some extent. Both emotional and physical changes occur. Nevertheless, the main takeaway from puberty is that your body can become pregnant. (This is not to say that you should, okay?)

Please be aware that there is a real danger of pregnancy when engaging in sexual activity, and that you should take responsible and safe sexual precautions.

Individual Routines

Daily Bath or Shower: During this stage, new sweat glands develop in your private areas and armpits, contributing to body odour. This is even more important for teenagers who participate in physical activities like sports. Always remember to apply deodorant following your daily shower and to quickly rinse off after working up a good sweat during an exercise or game.

Regular Hair Washing: Your hair becomes unclean. Indeed, it does. Additionally, some hormones might make your hair smell bad and be oily. You don't always need to shampoo your hair daily unless it gets unclean (like after sweating). This may potentially dry out and harm certain types of hair.

Inadequate hygiene is the primary cause of many skin illnesses. In addition, you can notice an increase in oiliness on your skin as you approach adolescence. Greasy skin provides a pathway for debris to get stuck. As part of your daily regimen, wash your face and use sunscreen to shield your skin from damaging UV radiation.

Haircuts and Brushing: Make sure you always brush your hair. The longer it is, the more styling it requires. Some varieties of hair can have split ends as their hair becomes longer. This means that the hair splits at the ends! It gives your hair a frizzed-out appearance, and getting a haircut preserves it strong and healthy!

Brush and Floss: Brushing twice daily helps eliminate pesky bacteria that produce foul breath and shields your teeth against illness.

Shave Often: (Obviously for guys) Hey, you're going to grow a beard or a moustache! Nice, huh? Cutting is a decision. If you decide to do so, clean your shaving supplies after each use.

Wear Clean garments: You should replace your underwear and garments daily. Unwanted odours will come from your body, releasing fluids that your clothing and underwear will retain. To avoid stinky feet, you should also change your socks daily. Gross!

Hand Wash Frequently: Dirty hands allow germs to spread fast. After using the restroom, before or after eating, and after you return from an excursion, wash your hands.

Nail care: Cleaning and routinely filing/cutting nails is part of caring for ourselves. Even if they are a haven for germs, you may like having long nails. Avoid negative behaviours as well, such as gnawing your fingernails.

There are tons of products available on the market to support your cleanliness. Advertisements encourage you to purchase the newest and greatest products to maintain a bright complexion and zit-free face. It could take a few purchases to discover your favourites. However, try to finish the product before purchasing the next one. Our bodies can take some time to adjust and learn what we like and dislike.

1.

Communication and behavior skills

An

You need to develop various talents as a teenager to succeed and successfully navigate adulthood. Behavioural skills are one type of these capabilities.

Effective communication, the development of positive relationships, job performance, and self-improvement are all made possible by behavioural skills.

Behavioural skills: what are they?

Behavioural skills include decision-making, responding appropriately to unforeseen events, and interacting with others.

Interpreting someone else's ideas, feelings, and behaviour is a skill anyone can employ.

The two most typical behavioural skill examples are:

Resolving conflicts

efficient exchange of ideas.

While some teenagers may be born with certain abilities, others may have to learn and grow to thrive and make their way through adulthood.

Behavioural Skills Examples

1. Interaction

Numerous communication abilities could be part of this behavioural competence, such as.

Engaging in active listening

Nonverbal exchanges, as well as the ability to think clearly.

Your ability to speak clearly and successfully as a teenager will be very helpful to you as you grow into adulthood. You'll need it for most of your adult life. Teens who are skilled communicators, for example, might listen intently to their tutors to understand assignment instructions.

These abilities will boost your productivity in the classroom and at work and confidence in any role.

2. Compassion

As a teenager, empathy is an essential behavioural ability because it allows you to understand other people's experiences, thoughts, and emotions.

Teens with empathy can understand the perspective of others and determine the potential reasons for it. For example, an exceptionally perceptive adolescent might notice that a friend appears nervous and asks if they need help.

Your ability to empathize could be used to work with individuals and put them at ease.

3. Time Administration.

As a teenager, time management is an essential behavioural skill that will help you flourish as an adult. It can benefit you both at work and in your academic endeavours.

Adolescents who are good time managers typically set objectives for themselves in life and figure out how to achieve them. They prioritize their tasks so that they can be sure to finish the most important tasks first.

They can also end distractions and concentrate fully on their task by using time management. Hence, as a teenager, behavioural skills boost productivity and efficiency.

4. Self-improvement.

Self-improvement skills help you identify areas where you may learn more to reach your objectives.

Adolescents who prioritize self-improvement are committed to learning new abilities that will help them and have a wide range of interests.

Using self-improvement approaches, you can enhance and build additional behavioural abilities that help you reach your goals in life.

5. Making choices.

Making decisions allows you to gather information, evaluate your options, and select the best action. It is an essential behavioural ability.

Though they may ask for advice or comments from others, teens who can make thoughtful decisions ultimately take ownership of their decisions and actions.

Decision-making is an important behavioural ability for teenagers who want to be in leadership roles since it allows them to make important choices for their group or organization.

Conclusion

Behavioural skills are important for your growth since they affect your attitude, conduct, and response in different situations.

These qualities influence how others perceive you personally, which can help you build and preserve connections at home, work, and in the classroom.

Gaining self-assurance through developing behavioural skills might motivate you to actively explore new hobbies and pastimes.

Safeguarding Your Money

A. Comprehending Insurance Coverage

Ensuring you have enough insurance to protect against unforeseen circumstances is part of protecting your finances. Insurance helps you reduce potential dangers by offering financial security and comfort. This chapter will address the value of having insurance, various insurance plans, and methods for assessing your insurance requirements.

1. The Value of Having Insurance

Insurance coverage is essential to safeguard your funds from unanticipated events that could cause large losses. When you most need financial support, insurance serves as a safety net. It assists with paying for emergency medical care, lost property, liability settlements, and other unforeseen expenses.

2. Insurance Coverage Types a. Health Insurance: You are shielded from excessive medical expenses by health insurance. Preventive care, prescription drugs, hospital stays, and doctor visits are all covered. Possessing health insurance guarantees that you can obtain essential medical services without facing crippling costs.

b. Auto Insurance: In the event of an accident, auto insurance protects you from liability and covers damage to your car. In most jurisdictions, it is legally required and offers financial protection against expensive repairs, medical expenses, and lawsuits brought about by mishaps.

C. Renters' and homeowners' insurance:

Against loss or damage in theft, fire, or natural catastrophes. Similar coverage is offered to tenants by renters insurance, which guards their personal property and their.

d. Life insurance: Should you pass away, this kind of insurance will financially support your loved ones. It supports burial costs, pays off outstanding obligations, and replaces lost income. You should consider getting life insurance if you have dependents who depend on your income.

e. Disability Insurance: It guarantees that even in the event of your incapacity to generate income, you can pay your bills and maintain your quality of living.

f. Liability Insurance: This type of insurance shields you from monetary damages brought about by lawsuits brought against you. It pays for losses and defence costs if you are found liable for accidents, property damage, or other obligations.

3. Assessing Your Needs for Insurance

Evaluating your insurance needs is critical to ensure you have the right coverage without paying too much for extraneous plans.

Consider your age, health, family, possessions, and possible hazards. Speak with insurance experts to assess your unique requirements and adjust coverage.

B. The Value of Estate Planning

Estate planning is essential to safeguard your finances and ensure your assets are handled and allocated according to your intentions. It entails arranging for your healthcare and final wishes and becoming ready to transfer your assets. This section will cover the significance of estate planning as well as important factors to take into account.

1. Safeguarding Your Resources and Preserving Memories Estate planning enables you to safeguard your resources and guarantee their allocation according to your wishes. Your assets can be vulnerable to probate without a suitable estate plan, which can be costly and time-consuming. Using estate planning, you can

also provide for your loved ones, such as young children or relatives with specific needs.

2. Important Estate Planning Components

a. Will: It names executors to oversee your inheritance, names beneficiaries for your belongings, and could even contain clauses about young children's guardianship. b. A trust is a formal structure in which assets are held and administered by a trustee on behalf of beneficiaries. Trusts can offer discretion, secrecy, and management of the distribution of assets. They can also help avoid probate and reduce estate taxes.

C. Power of Attorney: In the event of your incapacitation, a power of attorney gives someone you trust the right and ability to make financial or medical choices on your behalf. It guarantees that if you cannot do so.

d. Healthcare Directive/Living Will: These legal documents outline your desires for medical care and final disposition. It expresses your preferences for organ donation, life-sustaining procedures, and other medical decisions.

3. Collaborating with Experts

or estate planning lawyers may guarantee that your estate plan is thorough and compliant with the law. They may offer advice, assist you in navigating intricate legal procedures, and guarantee that your estate plan accurately reflects your goals and intentions.

C. Defending Against Theft of Identity

Safeguarding your data and avoiding identity theft are important aspects of financial protection. Identity theft happens when someone obtains unauthorized access to your financial accounts or commits fraud using your personal information. This section will cover the significance of safeguarding against identity theft and methods for improving your protection.

Section 1

Gaining a correct comprehension of oneself

You believe you understand yourself pretty well, but suddenly, you start behaving utterly against your nature, right?

Is it, though? Is it possible that your perception of who you are is inaccurate?

It's possible that the side of you does not entirely understand the unusual side of you in charge of everything else.

Whatever the case, your inherent weirdness keeps coming out.

Furthermore, you're unsure of whether to show who's in charge or try to work things out.

(And supposing that oddball turns out to be your boss?)

What, then, can you do to better understand who you are? Here are a few concepts.

1. Include daily journal writing in your regimen.

"Learning how to understand me" might be a fitting title for your diary.

Because every time you sit down to write in it, which will be quite frequent, you will have to do that.

Writing your daily journal entry will provide you with a playground for all the disorganized and connected ideas and thoughts circling around in your head, regardless of how much time you spend on it—five minutes, thirty minutes, or longer.

When you give kids a stage to perform their stories on, you notice those ideas more. Your brain receives a signal to pay attention when you write things down, and it complies.

As a result, these concepts are given more thought. Suddenly, you start to acknowledge things you had only half-consciously thought about until that moment.

Keeping this one anonymous will guarantee that it stays a safe space for people to vent. Everyone is obliged to have that.

2. Make it a habit to meditate every day.

You may become more anchored and receptive to the voice of your inner self by dedicating at least ten minutes a day to quiet meditation — five minutes at the start of the day and five minutes at the conclusion.

Meditating makes you break free from the mundane and self-centred world of your daily activities and ingrained thought patterns.

This strengthens your bond with your heart and, consequently, with your soul and all those connected to. to live without it if you allow this exercise to deepen your relationship with your shadow self.

3. Incorporate some thrills into your wish list.

Should you possess a bucket list, consider what items you may include on it that would cause you to feel slightly uneasy.

Take part in a task that pushes you much beyond your comfort zone.

Take part in public speaking in some capacity. Another possibility is stand-up comedy or karaoke.

You should not be scared to engage in scary activities and put yourself in potentially harmful circumstances, even if there are threats that the entire incident will be videotaped.

Particularly when someone has threatened to record the entire affair on video!

4. Develop a further creative skill.

Like me, you've probably always wondered why your mother loved knitting (or crocheting).

Alternatively, perhaps you've always had the desire to develop mobile applications.

If you discover that working on a certain creative project makes you feel more awake than five seconds ago, why not spend some time every week learning more about it?

Think about what you would like to accomplish for your first significant project, and then start by learning the skills required to move you closer to that objective.

Go forth and create something you can be proud of after that.

5. Attempt a more challenging task.

This idea is comparable to a bucket list, except it includes more spontaneous activities.

When someone invites you to give a speech, you clear your throat and approach the platform rather than bolting for the back door. Even if you're terrified, you're determined to seize the chance and accept the challenge.

Or perhaps your manager has asked someone else to lead a project that will probably put your skills to the test in every manner possible. And the fear of failing is the only thing keeping you from moving forward.

Staying in one's comfort zone is a wiser course of action. However, nothing ever develops there.

6. Have a more profound and meaningful conversation.

Make time in your calendar for longer, more in-depth conversations with the people who matter most to you.

Recognize any indications from their body language that they are going through emotional or mental distress and offer to be a listening ear.

And pay attention to what is being said rather than trying to outwit someone or prove that you are the expert on all problems.

Take advantage of this opportunity to deepen your comprehension of the other person.

This encounter will likely give you a better sense of who you are.

7. Obtain a personality assessment (such as the MBTI).

You ought to do so even if you have never taken the Myers-Briggs Type Indicator (MBTI).

It won't take long, and the outcomes can surprise you by illuminating facets of yourself that you might have noticed but not given much thought to.

You may seek guidance on choosing a career that will best reflect your true self and give you the most sense of aliveness.

Knowing your personality traits better can help you in numerous ways, and they are only hints.

You don't need to concur with every detail mentioned in the description of your sort. This one is best left to your intuition.

8. Take part in a conversational game.

The next time you get together with friends or go on a date with someone you're seeing seriously, try playing a discussion game.

Generally, you will be asked questions to which you will have to give honest answers without any space for self-doubt.

It's possible that what you say will seem unbelievable to you.

Additionally, if it starts a lively conversation, seize the opportunity to learn more about the other person, participants, and yourself.

To restate, the objective is to increase one's knowledge rather than to obtain an advantage at the expense of another.

2. SET SMALL, SMART GOALS FOR YOURSELF.

Highlights the need to precisely and measurably state your financial goals.

You can establish measurable and well-defined objectives by setting explicit goals. You have to be very clear about what you hope to accomplish. Clear and precise objectives can be achieved, for instance, by aiming for goals like purchasing a home, paying off debt, saving for emergencies, or hitting a particular income threshold.

By establishing quantifiable objectives, you may monitor your development and assess your achievement based on certain standards. This entails having precise metrics or measurements that you may use to assess your progress and make any required corrections. Measurable goals offer concrete benchmarks that may be used to track advancement, such as saving a certain amount of money or earning a certain return on investment.

Establishing quantifiable, explicit goals will help you stay motivated and focused on your financial goals. These objectives provide you with a precise road map and let you monitor your development. They also help you become more focused and accountable for reaching your objectives.

To sum up, having specific, quantifiable goals will aid you in achieving financial success. With the help of these objectives, you may keep yourself motivated, monitor your progress, and precisely define your aims. You can succeed more readily if you take deliberate action to meet your financial objectives.

3. MONITOR YOUR EXPENSES AND GET BUDGET AWARENESS

Understanding where your money is going and what you spend it on requires tracking it. It enables you to take control of your financial position by helping you comprehend it. Keeping track of your spending aids in creating a thorough budget and assists in identifying wasteful spending.

It's possible to balance your income and expenses by developing a budget. One technique for managing your income and expenses is a budget. You can figure out how much you need to set aside for necessities by defining your income precisely. Budgeting lets you save money, cut debt, and control finances.

Setting financial objectives for the future is another benefit of budgeting. Within your budget, you could, for instance, give priority to investing, paying off debt, or saving. Understanding how to create a budget helps you make the right decisions to reach your financial objectives.

You may manage your money more skillfully and develop financial discipline by keeping track of your spending and creating a budget. It keeps your finances in check, promotes saving, and assists you in identifying wasteful expenditures. It also offers direction for accomplishing your future financial objectives.

Are critical to your financial success. By doing these actions, you may stay in control of your finances, comprehend your current financial condition, and progress toward your long-term objectives. A budget is a strong instrument for ensuring financial stability and wise money management.

4. TO GROW YOUR INCOME, SELECT NEW SKILLS OR IMPROVE ONES YOU ALREADY HAVE.

Raising your income gives you more financial alternatives and allows you to move closer to your financial objectives more quickly. Thus, developing new abilities or improving ones you already have is a key strategy for raising your income.

Acquiring new abilities may lead to greater career prospects. You can become more competitive in a wider employment market by learning new languages, improving your technological skills, or learning marketing tactics. You may be able to access greater career prospects, increasing your income.

Improving your skill set makes you more employable in your current position or sector. This may result in prospects for advancement or better pay. For example, enhance your technical proficiency or strengthen your sense of responsibility and establish yourself as a valuable asset in the company.

Acquiring fresh abilities or improving current ones also allows you extra revenue. You can diversify your income sources by, for instance, beginning freelancing in a field where you have a knack or area of expertise or by turning your interests into extra cash. This may help to improve your financial stability.

In conclusion, improving your abilities or picking up new ones to earn more money helps you succeed financially. By following these procedures, you can improve your career prospects, find new sources of income, and progress in your existing position. You may accomplish your financial objectives more quickly and have a better financial future by raising your income.

Set aside money for sporadic costs.

Certain expenses, like those for Christmas, are sporadic. Determine the total amount you spend on them over a year and divide it by 12. You can save this money monthly until the bill or expense is due.

Utilize money

You can better manage your expenditures if you use cash. Leave your debit card at home, when you shop, or on a day out. Because you can only spend what you have, you won't exceed your budget in this method.

Set a limit on your out-of-budget expenses.

The amount left over after deducting expenses from income is known as net income, an important component of your budget. You can spend the remaining money, up to a specific amount, on leisure and pleasure. This money isn't enough to go crazy with, especially because it must last a month. Make sure a large purchase won't conflict with your other plans before making it.

in your forties

Open an online retirement calculator and determine if you're now on track for your desired retirement age of about twenty years. If you're not making enough money, start examining your spending (and lifestyle) to identify areas where you may cut costs. Most financial gurus advise having two to three times your yearly salary saved in retirement funds by the time you are in your 40s.

Cold-hearted to put retirement ahead of tuition expenses? Callous? Not if you work with your child to prioritize financially fit schools. Hint: It's all about the net price, which you can calculate without taking money out of your retirement account or reducing your savings. This lowers the likelihood that the children may require your retirement support.

Avoid lifestyle creep: You may earn more money now than in your 20s, but are you spending it all?

fifty years old

Here are some figures to consider: experts advise saving six times your pay by the time you are 50. Save seven times your wage by the time you're 55.

Determine how much monthly income you can securely create using one of the many online calculators available.

Think about hiring an expert to help with the strategy: You could like saving for retirement on your own. However, considering all the components of creating a good retirement income plan, you might think about working through your retirement income plan with a professional financial planner. Many planners bill by the hour or on a set rate basis for a particular task. Alternatively, you might want to consider hiring an expert to assist you with managing your funds after retirement.

Benefit from catch-up contributions: The yearly contribution limits for 401(k)/403(b) and IRA plans increase as you reach the half-century mark, also known as the retirement savings Rubicon. Put extra money into your accounts immediately if an online retirement income calculator doesn't give you the desired results.

Increase tax diversification: If the majority of your employment retirement savings have been placed in traditional accounts, you might want to think about investing for a few years in a Roth comparable account, should your plan have one. Experts in retirement planning advise putting some money into a Roth retirement account to generate "tax diversification," which will help you pay less in taxes after retirement.

in your sixties

Verify if these figures add up: Save eight times your wage by the time you're 60. Save ten times your wage by the time you're 67.

Think twice before claiming Social Security benefits. At age 62, you can begin receiving your retirement income. You will eventually receive a larger reward each month you wait past 62. Your compensation will be 76% greater if you wait until 70 years old than if you make your claim eight years earlier.

Make just enough money to prevent beginning withdrawals from your retirement account: It's fantastic if you can and want to keep working a fast-paced, full-time job.

However, even though you can't afford to keep adding to your retirement funds, working at a job that pays enough to cover your living expenses might be a sensible move if you're ready to downshift or were forced out of your profession. It makes sense to wait until after you have had more time to allow your savings to multiply to begin taking withdrawals from your savings.

The Benefits of Monitoring Your Spending

Do you frequently ponder where your money disappears? Keeping track of your spending.

There are numerous ways to keep track of your spending, including sophisticated software, smartphone apps, and the old-fashioned pen-and-paper method. This chapter will examine the most widely used techniques and provide advice on streamlining and expediting the procedure.

Conventional Pen and Paper

One of the earliest and most basic ways to track your spending is to list every item you buy and every expense you incur in a notebook or spreadsheet. With this strategy, you may track your spending over time and categorize your expenses by category.

Despite being low-tech, this method can be time-consuming and demands discipline. On the other hand, the advantages of observing your spending trends in writing are that it.

Spreadsheets in Excel

Spreadsheets in Excel are a popular and configurable tool for keeping track of spending. You can budget and keep real-time tabs on your expenses with Excel. You can organize your spending into categories, make graphs and charts to see how much you spend, and set up alerts to tell you when you're about to exceed your allotted spending limit.

Excel is a fantastic choice if you want a customized solution and are comfortable using technology. It might not be as portable as other solutions, though, and it takes some effort to set up initially.

Smartphone Applications

Mobile apps have revolutionized our ability to track costs. These days, many free or inexpensive apps may assist you with budgeting and tracking your expenses. You can easily examine your spending in real time with these applications, which you can access from your tablet or smartphone.

Mobile apps are a fantastic choice for people who are constantly on the go and need to track their costs from any location. They might send you alerts when you're getting close to your spending limit. Nevertheless, until you upgrade to a paid version, some apps might only operate partially or require a subscription.

Internet Resources

Online resources are yet another well-liked choice for cost tracking. You can instantly track your spending and link all of your accounts in one location with the help of a plethora of websites and online applications. Over time, set financial objectives and develop budgets.

Online tools are a smart choice if you want a single area to store your financial data. They allow you to keep an eye on all your accounts in one location and can reveal information about your spending habits. Nevertheless, until you upgrade to a paid version, some online tools might only operate partially or require a subscription.

Some Good Expense-Tracking Advice

Here are some pointers to help you get the most out of keeping track of your spending:

Maintain coherence: No matter how tiny the purchase, keep track of it all and accurately categorize your expenses to obtain a clear picture of your spending patterns.

Regularly review your expenditures: Allocate a specific period every week or month to examine your expenditures and pinpoint any instances where you may be overspending. This will assist you in modifying your spending plan and maintaining your financial objectives.

Make the most of technology and tools: make expense tracking simpler and more efficient, regardless of your preference for a more conventional method or a cutting-edge smartphone app.

To sum up, keeping track of your spending is an effective way to manage your money. It might assist you in locating areas in which you are overspending and modifying your spending plan. You can get financial control and reach your goals by selecting an approach that suits you and heeding this advice.

www.ingramcontent.com/pod-product-compliance
Lightning Source LLC
Chambersburg PA
CBHW052150110526
44591CB00012B/1918